Spring Poems for a New World

for a

A Book of Poems

MARK S. JONES

Print information available on the last page

Rev. date: 05/27/2015

To order additional copies of this book, contact:
Xlibris
1-888-795-4274
www.Xlibris.com
Orders@Xlibris.com

Foreword

This is a compilation of new and old Poems and photos I put together in the first 5 months of 2015. About 11 of the Poems are Fresh out of my Heart written in the year of our Lord, 2015. The older poems are oldies but goodies and have proved to be True over Time! My Publisher assures me that they are aiming to make the Book 100 % perfect and I Believe it Will take Wings and FLY!

I want to Thank My Mom Sheila, Father, Richard who Art in Heaven, the Publishers at Xlibris, Jesus, many Friends on facebook, my Cats: Ernie and Mona, for not stepping on my computer keys too much and the Many Life Teachers and Poets I have had to Bless me in my Writing Life! Bless you Readers and I hope you enjoy my latest Book of Poetry!

Sincerely,

Mark Stephen Jones May 18, 2015

Acknowledgements

I want to thank my Mother-Sheila, my father Richard,

God- Jesus, many great teachers and coaches I had with my life, 2 wives, and a girlfriend of 20 years that still remain nameless, the US Army and VA system which I read many of my Poems to, Marylou McClure an inspirational leader at the VA Medical Center Seattle WA. I also want to thank my 2 cats, Ernie- Marcus and Mona Lisa for cooperating while I prepared this book.

I also want to thank my Grandparents Florence and Dr. Read Bain; and Helen Jones and William Jones who encouraged me and without them I could not have written this.

Mark Stephen Jones

May 2015

Spring Morning Poems

Why did you have to go,

Did you choose the time and the hour,

Did you know how sad I would be?

You know I would have saved you again,

If it was in my power...

Transition:

You brought the true Spring as you made your Transition,
You left us with True Warmth 1 month into Spring,
My tears finally come, now that you are gone,
And yet in some ways you are more Present than ever...
You are more Spring than Winter and you Loved Well,
I take a breath for you and I am glad I never said goodbye,
For Good....

Minds Eye

In My Minds Eye I see you, hammer in hand doing Mans Work,

All I could figure out to do was Play, I was only five,
And yet I wanted to help you, be like you,

I wanted to be strong, I wanted to help...

And Later I did, I was Life Saver, I saved your Life.

Or was that just how it was meant to be?

In my Minds Eye I saw you in your Tent in the
Meadow reading Keats and Shelley,

After I had experienced another setback,

I SAW YOU BY THE River as the bonfire blazed
and wondered why you were not cold?

Later I saw your Cheeks Shining And your "Glow"

That no one could take from you...

In My Minds Eye again I saw you with your hammer in your hand,

I thought Of John Henry beating the Steam Drill,

Now I have the Hammer...

For my Dad Richard G. Jones March 18, 1927- April 18, 2007...

Lived 80 years and 1 month blessing to him in the "Transition" Amen...

Mark Stephen Jones 4/21/2007 in the morning...

Happy Brithday July 2007

You are a Great Gift to Humankind and to me,

Your listening skill is A-1 helping me to see,

That I can let "it" be, that I can really be free...

Once Again...

This time with Greater Wisdom, Knowing that the loneliness will

Soon pass and I could fall for some Lass,

You are much like a Mirror, but a Caring Mirror if you will,

I like you and care about you and enjoy your Wit,

I feel fortunate that it was You I got, yes You and not another,

It feels right and hey are you making progress they say?

Well not in the way you normally think of progress,

That is, the Results are Lived Out and not all ways measurable,

I am thankful you are there, that you are who you are Now!

I think You Are Love, my Friend, in your own Quiet Way,

You came to be with me; today,

It is an Honor, one that I would not trade away!

I feel a bit stuck because I do not want to leave,
but someday I may have to go,

The worst of "it" is over but I am still moving kind of slow....,

I want you to know you have helped me to Grow!

Happy Birthday Robin, May you have a Great Year!!,

When I see you at Starbucks I will raise up a Cheer!,

For You, the Master of Love and Overcomer of fear!!

Thank you for your Great Work on my Life Journey!!...

Mark Stephen Jones 7-27-2007

Lots of 7's!

Love Again

I won't let you say goodbye completely, You think
you solved your dilemma so neatly,

You seem to expand your space; of your Love there is no trace,

But you will grow and you will know, When it feels right to Love Again,

And when you're strong and when You Care,
You will see that again you Can Share,

You found loss is hard and money soothes, but Your heart must heal,

So that no one can attempt to steal it, like I did, Perhaps I tried to Hard?

And though it was the World Series, I think
I ran out of room, Forgive Me?

MSJ 6/5/2009

Time

The Time has come for you to See, Just what our love was meant to be,

Love cannot end, it is shared, rises, I miss You or I miss the ME,

That me of previous sizes,

I shall see him again and there will be new surprises!

MSJ 6/5/2009

Light Rain

Light Rain take away my pain,

Give me new energy so true,

I've been down and weak,

No love do I seek,

I feel oh so meek....

I don't wish to suffer or sigh,

I would rather Live than die,

But my Heart is so sad,

Because I want something bad,

And I can't figure out what that something is ?

MSJ 3/27/2009

Another Woman Coming?

Lord tell me if a Woman is Coming?

Or are you giving me a long time out?

I don't want a woman to be just another bad habit,

I want her to inspire me and I want to inspire her!

I don't want a trophy to hang on my wall....

But help her to have the kind of beauty that is
special only to me and you and my cats...

Send me that woman when the time is right...please....

Who said anything about marriage?

Thank You!

Outside my condo on a snowy day

My cat Ernie at my garden

My friend Josh and Ernie

POEM #99 (2000-2007)

The Farm Boy made it to the big city,

Where the Lights were bright and Girls were Pretty,

He could not get a square meal however,

No Job, No satisfying endeavour,

So he brought it all back home to the farm,

Where he would do nobody harm,

And soon worked hard each day,

With fresh produce as his pay,

Chased the city blues away!

MSJ August 2007 from City- Country-City

My Little Butterfly

She said remember the Butterfly and I thought why?

Just when I thought she was content to let our love die,

I told myself I was "letting go" and I couldn't, now I can,

Yet I am sure I am not the same man!

I am growing in ways I cannot control,

And I feel like a lonely, happy, Soul..

She said remember the Butterfly and I wonder why?

Just when it seemed our Love was about to die,

And ofcourse I do wish her Well,

God Bless her and if the Butterfly comes back,

Please Ring a Bell!

MSJ April 13,2006

Death

Death took my Grandma today,

I wish she could stay,

In this life with me,

But she's gone and finally free,

Of all the worlds pain,

Of all the worlds gain,

She was a good woman and I see,

That she meant a whole lot to me.

MSJ 13th of April '89

Am I a Poet?

My grandmother told me to keep a hand in,

Now where do I begin?

She said to work on meter too,

And that I still need to do.

Grandma always had an encouraging word,

Making me want to soar like a bird.

Poetry is food for the soul,

Allowing you to reach your highest goal.

Am I a Poet?

Well you know it.

Mark thinking of Grandma Florence Davis Bain 2/22/91

Blue Sky

Blue Sky all around,

Blue sky and sunshine lights up the town,

It is cold and clear and blue,

Like me it is Blue and it is True,

I know I'll be okay by and by,

I can find love again if I try,

For now I'll enjoy the blue sky,

And Live before I die!

MSJ 2-4-2010

Frozen in Time

I remember when I called you with my last dime,

Since then,

Now and again, I have felt Frozen in Time,

My anchor gone, my boat had no direction,

Ended up singing the same old rhyme,

As if I was Frozen in Time...

Frozen in Time, where the good loving stopped,

Frozen in Time where your last memory fades,

Frozen in Time, where I miss you Babe

And where my clock ran out of time....

Where I still wish you were mine....

MSJ 4/30/2010

My mother Sheila holding smoked salmon around year 2000

The Coffee is Strong

The Coffee is strong,

So people don't stay as long,

They get their buzz,

And off they Go,

Very Fast, not at all Slow,

The Coffee is Strong,

All Day Long...

MSJ 10/9/2006

Going to see Momma

Going to see Momma,

At the place she stays,

Hope that we cheer her up on the Rainy Days,

I'm sure she'll be fine in a while,

And it will be nice

To see her smile!

MSJ 10/19/2009

Life Goes On

Every waking moment is precious and so is your love, Love!

I am not a fan of the hawk, but of the Peace Dove,

I rejoice because of every moment I've had to share and will share with you,

To the Spirit of Love, I am True Blue!

MSJ 1/9/2015

My World + Your World = Our World

I have to dream Sara, because it must be
a better Dream than this in heaven,

There seems to be no magic formulas,

I need a place to call my own again, my room,

Far north and at the back, where solitude and
quiet can be the rule once again,

Like my dad so many times said, "Your Life is not your Own"!

And indeed...indeed, it is not...

MSJ 1/2015

Meditation Poem

Turn off your mind and breathe,

Letting the Universe breathe you,

Send good vibes from your Soul,

Receive Good vibes from the Universe

Send Good vibes to the Universe

Breathe the Universe into good fortune,

Match your will with Gods,

Empty any toxicity into the disappearing black hole,

See the Light, feel the Warmth,

Give and Receive and Give,

You are Love!

MSJ 5/28/2009

The Sun Shines

The sun shines bright,

And it blinds my sight,

I loved 4 women with all my might,

Make that 5 and I am lucky to be Alive!

I paid the price of solitude,

And to the road less taken,

I ate brown rice and gave up bacon,

I have loved and lost, loved and lost,

All at Great cost,

Part wishing I was Gatsby or

Redford, at least,

Bossed around by tiny men

And beauties now deceased.

Bought Freud, Maslow and Dylan,

Kerouac, and Thoreau, Rembrant and Van Gogh,

Now there is no one I really owe

Except maybe my sweet Momma and not even her, but God, yes, now I
want to go on Loving God, and I don't think that is odd,

After all that I have been through, How about you ?!

MSJ 2/18/2015

Two of my best friends from childhood Ron Wong and Claire Wilson

Friends from Roosevelt H.S. 40th year reunion

The Fight of the Century

Muhammad Ali's 2nd fight with Joe Frazier
(Madison Square Garden 1973)

It was the Fight of the Century,

A test of might,

To see who would not just talk, but could really fight,

The bets were all set and would soon see,

Who was really the Champ, Big Joe or Ali?

It was the night of the fight,

And "Bong" went to the bell,

The fans were excited and started to yell!

Both fighters fought hard all over the Ring,

Each determined to prove he was King,

But in the 11th Muhammad got slow, tired
and weary taking blow after blow,

He fought back like a champion with his old poise and grace,

Only to be floored be a left to the face!

Spring 2015

As the daffodils and tulips rise

To meet the on coming Spring,

I thank God for Poetry and the chance to Sing,

Love knocks again at the door of my heart,

The Sun smiles on me and my Art,

I have changed my Heart,

And God blesses my step

The blue sky indicates there is a clearing, there is Love, endearing,

There is a message worth hearing,

I turn my head to the mountains and the sky,

I see my Lover, again, in My mind's eye!

MSJ 03/19/2015

Fishing boat at La Conner, Washington

My spring garden: tulips and forget-me-not

Poem for the Lord and Me

Thy will be done Lord and I

Know you know what I need,

Be with me Lord,

I am your child, your son,

Be with me Jesus,

The Day has just begun!

Be with me Lord, help me keep my Cool,

Help me remember the Golden Rule.

Help me take my time and think, Jesus,

Lord help me get it Right,

Be with me Lord and those I meet!

MSJ 11/23/12

I am Best at Poetry

If I am at a loss for Words,

And long to fly with the birds,

When I gaze upon the inward eye,

That is the bliss of Solitude,

I dance as Wordsworth did with the daffodils,

The Creator loves me I know,

I feel the Great Spirit as I help my Garden Grow,

The Spiritual Life agrees with me you know,

Celibate as I am, My love is Power,

Above and beyond any problem I can tower,

With God's Love I feel Bliss,

And cherish my kittens hug and kiss,

I do not fear because I know,

God's Love is here!

MSJ 3-20-2015

Spring is Here!

If it were not for my Cats I would be sad,

After all the Love lost and found I've had,

I knocked on Heavens door,

And experienced Life to the full,

I've seen God's work and felt his pull.

I've been pleased to write and share my verse,

Rhymed in time, chimed in, lost kin,

Felt love and pain within,

Played my Song on Guitar,

Gazed at Venus and a Shooting Star,

Read my share and I'll read some more,

Now in 2015 I shall Roam,

And I'll be Happy when I end up Home!

MSJ 3/20/2015

The Poet

37

Ocean Shores Washington at sundown

Good friends at the high school reunion

Printed in the United States
By Bookmasters